BonkaWonkaGonka

Sarah Ingram

Siena Rumbough

Hello Saris

THIS BOOK BELONGS TO:

BonkaWonkaGonka

Copyright © 2022 by Helper Tees, LLC.
For general information about Helper Tees and their products:
www.helpertees.com

Interior and Cover Design: Hello Saris
Authors: Sarah Ingram & Siena Rumbough
Production Editor: Siena Rumbough
Production Manager: Helper Tees, LLC.

Hardcover ISBN: 978-0-578-29266-3
eBook ISBN: 978-0-578-29267-0

LCCN: 2022913618

Health Education, Self-Care, Emotional Intelligence, Conscious Parenting, ABC's, 123's, Nutrition,
Big Emotions, Bathtime, Bedtime Story, Children's Book, Routine

Printed and Bound in the U.S.A.
First Published in 2022

**Dedicated to the reader
of this book.**

You're doing an amazing job, and you truly
don't hear it enough!

A Special Note to Readers:

We're thrilled you're here! Thank you for choosing us to be a part of your little one's journey towards "sunshine all over inside." Our emotions are sending our bodies a message. As such, we created this book as a tool to help you empower your littles towards exploring their BIG emotions and learning what helps them feel better.

At Helper Tees, we believe our minds and bodies work together!
One of our favorite lines in this book is:

"My body and mind can connect to feel better, We'll show you what happens when the two work together:"

It's an empowering feeling when both our minds and bodies can support one another to feel good. So, what does that look like? We've learned that routines can be very helpful for our littles to feel more grounded.
When we know what to expect, we have more space to process big feelings along the way. Let your littles take the lead on establishing a fun self-care routine outside of this book, and don't forget to schedule joy into your days!

Complete with beautiful and memorable illustrations that will guide your little reader along, this book explores how a big blue feeling can turn to sunshine! Follow throughout Bonka's day as his best friend, Stori, encourages him to listen to his body to address his immediate needs and, as a result, his big blue. Bonka quickly learns the importance of routine and having a plan to calm his BIG emotions. Just as Bonka was lucky to have Stori guide him through, your littles are lucky to have you!

Thank you for sharing this book with the little ones in your life. We hope Bonka inspires a new love for self-care, pinpointing feelings, and ultimately, shining as our best selves.

You'll find the more you read, the more there will be to discover and chat about!

We hope you enjoy this story as much as we loved bringing it to life.

Love,
Your Bonka Family

Hi, friends!

My name is **BonkaWonkaGonka.**
First, you start by saying **'Bonka,'**
Then you add the **'Wonka,'**
And you finish with the **'Gonka.'**

Bonka-Wonka-Gonka.

BONKA-WONKA-GONKA

I woke up with big, big feelings today,
I have a great blueness that won't go away!
This happens to everyone once in a while,
All shades of blue feelings that I can turn to a smile.

I'll pause for deep breathing, then hop UP for self-care,
I'll label my feelings, each and every one there!

I can be happy, sleepy, or sad,
Sometimes I'm **bored**,
surprised
or **big mad**.

Feelings come and go, I know this, it's true.
But to feel my very best, I'll try a self-care practice or two!

My adventure will start with my daily routine!
Taking care of my body and keeping it clean.

I'll invite my best friend to share in the glory,
She's kind and smart, and she goes by **"Stori."**
Everything is better with her by my side;
What a day it will be with my self-care guide!

My body and mind can connect to feel better,
We'll show you what happens when the two work together:

My teeth feel sticky and icky.
I should brush them, let me see,
What do I need to make the sugar bugs flee?!
Bubblegum toothpaste! YES, that is the key!

Brush Bonka,
Brush Wonka,
Don't rush, Gonka!

Let's wash it away, **KERSPLAT!** in the sink,
They shine oh so bright, you'll be sure to blink!

My teeth feel happy, it's true,
But I still feel this

big, big, big blue.

I'll jump out of my clothes and into the bath,
I'll even use my magical soap to practice my math!

We'll rinse this big blue right down with a scrub,
ZONK! Go all my toys, **KERPLOP** in the tub.

To keep this all straight,
I'll make this big list,
With all these fun toys, you cannot resist:

1 rubber duck,
2 blue and red trucks,
3 mermaids from the ocean,
4 bottles with secret potions, and
5 choo-choo trains!

1, 2, 3, 4, 5!

I counted to five. Great job, brain!

GROWL!

A rumble comes from my tummy.
I know what will fix it, something delicious, something yummy.
Maybe something purple, definitely something green,
To keep my bones healthy, and my mind sharp and keen!

GROOOWL

VOILA!

Is it a rainbow, or is it my plate?!
Stori, let's eat this colorful food before it's too late!

Wait! Wait!

Zoom to the bathroom I go.
I wash my hands with foamy soap until they glow.
Sing a song, or say a rhyme,
But I'll spell my name to track the time.

B-O-N-K-A-W-O-N-K-A-G-O-N-K-A.

Wow,
It's a long name, it's true.
But to show we love our bodies,
We wash the germs away, too.
I wash my hands throughout the day—
That way, I am healthy and I can go play.

RAWR!

Goes my tummy,
Now it's time for that something yummy.

I like **coconut**,

bananas,

and
avocado toast;

 I like **figs**

 and **oranges,**

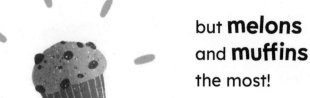 but **melons**
and **muffins**
the most!

My tummy is full, and I'm feeling better; I do!
Nourishing my body, I feel a little less blue.

It's time to get dressed and into my shoes,
Let's go outside and get rid of the rest of these blues!
When it's hard to explain what this blue is inside,
That's when I let exercise be my guide.

With a **Bonka,** and a **Wonka,** and a **Gonka,**

I GO!

Ready for any weather:
rain, sleet, shine or **snow.**

I'll play, and I'll play,
And I'll play all day long.

But wait! Even after all this fun,
Something seems wrong.

I have wiggles and giggles trapped in my toes!
I feel them inside from my feet to my nose!

POW!

Get them out,
I'll ride my bike until these wiggles won't make me shout.

Aww.

Thank you, Stori; through all this I grew.
Having a plan helped calm this big blue.

I thought this blueness was stuck inside,
A big, big, big blue, ten elephants wide.

But now I feel sunshine all over inside,
A big, big, big happy, **twelve** elephants wide,

So with a **Bonka**, and a **Wonka**, and a **Gonka**, I GO!
To bed for now; there's still so much more to grow.

Resources page

Congratulations! You're officially part of the **BONKA FAMILY**. We're so happy you're in our close-knit community! To say "thank you," we want to offer you some fun and helpful free resources.

Begin by navigating to:

www.HelperTees.com

Here you will find access to countless **FREE PDF** resources that foster a love of self-care, exercise your littles' ABC's and 123's, offer nutritious snack options, and most of all, help your little one grow in emotional intelligence—just like Bonka and Stori! Not only are these educational, but they are beautiful to hang around your home!

We are continually updating Helper Tees with educational tools, so be sure to check back often.

Continue the conversation with your littles:

⭐ **"What activities help you feel sunshine all over inside?"**
⭐ **"What is one self-care activity we can add to our day together?"**
⭐ **"What was your favorite part of the book? Why?"**
⭐ **"Thank you for being you. You are so special and important to me. I loved reading this book with you."**
⭐ **Don't forget to color Bonka on the next page!**

We hope you loved this book as much as we loved bringing it to life!

-Your Bonka Family

Color Bonka!